Train To Essex Junction

A Play in One Act

By
David S. Traub Jr.

Cover design by Erika Phoenix

ISBN: 979-8-8692-7171-6

academyartspress.com

All Rights Reserved
Copyright © 2024, by David S. Traub Jr.

DAVID S. TRAUB, JR.

Train To Essex Junction
A Play in One Act
By
David S. Traub Jr.

In Order of Appearance

Jim Byrnes	A 62-year-old Train Barman
Stephen Logan	A 59-year-old Financier
Jennifer	A strait-laced Librarian, early Forties
Agnes	A self-proclaimed 'Free Spirit,' late Thirties
Announcer	Voice-over from the train's PA system

Scene One	Stephen Meets Jim in an Amtrak Train Café Car
Scene Two	Jennifer Enters Café Car
Scene Three	Agnes Enters Café Car, Jennifer Leaves
Scene Four	Agnes, Stephen & Jim Together, Agnes Leaves
Scene Five	Stephen and Jim Alone Together

All five scenes take place in the Café Car of an Amtrak Train. The play's action covers a ten-hour train ride from Pennsylvania to Vermont. The length of the play as performed is a little over one hour.

Train To Essex Junction
A Play in One Act
By
David S. Traub Jr.

*For royalty information and permission to use this play
in a performance, please email
vin@academyarts.com
with the following information:*

*Theater Name, City & State
Production Dates & Number of Performances
Ticket Prices & Number of seats
School, Community Theater or
Professional Company
Artistic Director and Contact Information*

We will contact you promptly by email

DAVID S. TRAUB, JR.

*THE PLAY IS DEDICATED IN MEMORY OF THE PLAYWRIGHT'S FATHER,
DR. DAVID S. TRAUB, SR. (1910-1965)*

A PRACTITIONER OF INTERNAL MEDICINE
IN LOUISVILLE, KENTUCKY AND AN EARLY SPECIALIST
IN THE TREATMENT OF DIABETES.

MEDICAL CONSULTANT TO THE PLAYWRIGHT
DR. MARSHALL PRIMACK, NEW YORK CITY.

SUGGESTED MUSIC FOR THE PLAY:

"THIS TRAIN" - SISTER ROSETTA THARP,
1964 RECORDING

"NIGHT TRAIN" - THE OSCAR PETERSON TRIO,
1963 RECORDING

"THE TRAIN AND THE RIVER" – JIMMY GIUFFRE,
1957 RECORDING

SCENE ONE

AT RISE. Lights come up on the interior of an Amtrak train car traveling from Philadelphia to Vermont. The train car is seen on the stage as if sliced lengthwise down the center with the cafe counter to the left and rows of booth tables marching to the right down from the bar. As the scene opens, no one is behind the counter. The barman – JIM, 62, sits alone at an adjacent booth-like table, munching on a sandwich. He wears a train porter vest, white shirt and a red tie, and is staring off into space.

ANNOUNCER. *(Voice Over)* Now leaving Philadelphia Station.

(After a few moments, STEPHEN, 59, enters, wearing a summer business suit in a light shade, a white shirt, a brightly colored stripped tie, and a white pocket square handkerchief in his jacket pocket (no vest.) He looks around the empty train car, then approaches the bar. He sees there is no one behind the bar, and turns to Jim.)

STEPHEN. Good morning, sir. May I have a cup of coffee?

JIM. The bar is closed.

STEPHEN. At eight-thirty in the morning?

JIM. I said the bar is closed.

STEPHEN. Why's that?

JIM. You heard what I said?

STEPHEN. I did.

JIM. Well, good.

STEPHEN. You seem quite comfortable sitting there...with your sandwich. I'll tell you what. I'll just plunk down here and read this Amtrak travel magazine.

JIM. You do that...

(Stephen sits down in the booth behind Jim.)

STEPHEN. I don't know why you're acting that way. All I want, sir, is a cup of coffee. Is that too much to ask?

JIM. *(Without looking up)* Right now, that's askin' a lot.

STEPHEN. I find that a little hard to understand, Mr...?

JIM. Byrnes

STEPHEN. Mr. Byrnes, you don't have to get all huffy. I've been rushing to make the train. Didn't have time for breakfast.

JIM. Do tell.

STEPHEN. I just did.

JIM. Yeah, guys like you are always rushing.

STEPHEN. Guys like me? What do you mean 'guys like me?'

JIM. Look at that suit you're wearing. People don't dress up on these trains.

STEPHEN. Just habit.

JIM. Bet you can't break that one.

STEPHEN. Maybe I don't want to.

JIM. *(Shrugs)* That's up to you.

STEPHEN. Right.

JIM. And you don't seem the kind to be taking a train. Well, maybe the Acela.*

---

*The Acela is the expensive, high-speed train operated by Amtrak.

STEPHEN. As a matter of fact, I do take the Acela a couple times a week...to Manhattan. And Mr. Byrnes, you should know, I like trains; have since I was a kid. I find them relaxing, and in fact, I'm in no hurry today. *(Pause)* Well, true, I was rushing this morning. But now I am just going to sit here in the cafe car for the whole ten hours it takes to get up to Essex Junction.

JIM. So, you're going to Vermont, huh?

STEPHEN. Thought I would have a little vacation where it's cooler. Besides, I have an old friend up there I haven't seen for years.

JIM. I'm guessin' another guy like you.

STEPHEN. There you go again with that stuff.

JIM. I'll try to hold off.

STEPHEN. I would appreciate that.

JIM. So, why do you go to Manhattan every week?

STEPHEN. I work in finance. I have an office in Philadelphia, but I have business on Wall Street too.

JIM. Ahhh, ok, now it all makes sense.

STEPHEN. Mr. Byrnes. What the hell? I don't really know you, and you for sure don't know me. Might it be possible to cut the rattle, once and for all?

JIM. Might as well. My break is over.

(Jim rises and moves back behind the bar counter.)

STEPHEN. Now that you're back on the job, perhaps I can get that cup of coffee?

JIM. Sure. Come and get it.

STEPHEN. On my way.

(Stephen crosses to the bar.)

JIM. Anything else you want?

STEPHEN. No, just coffee. Black.

JIM. You got it.

> *(Jim hands him the cup of coffee. Stephen takes a sip.)*

STEPHEN. Nice 'n hot.

JIM. Glad you like it.

> *(Stephen continues sipping his coffee and looks back over the train car.)*

STEPHEN. Say, why is this car so empty? It's just you and me.

JIM. This run don't get many passengers during the week. Probably more coming on when we reach New York.

STEPHEN. The quiet is kind of nice...now that I have my coffee.

JIM. So you're happy.

STEPHEN. Finally am.

> *(Stephen returns to his seat. Jim hovers at the bar, straightening things up for a few moments then returns to the booth in front of Stephen.)*

JIM. I'll just sit down and take it easy. If someone comes on, I'll scurry back.

STEPHEN. What's the old line; take care of business before pleasure?

JIM. Pleasure? Ha!

STEPHEN. Mr. Byrnes. It's going to be a long trip. Do I have to hear more of this stuff? I just want to enjoy myself.

JIM. That's what passengers are supposed to do.

STEPHEN. That's what I thought...

> *(A long pause. Music is heard.)*

STEPHEN. Mr. Byrnes, can I ask you something?

JIM. Yeah, what?

STEPHEN. Where are you from?

JIM. Baltimore.

STEPHEN. Nice town.

JIM. You think so?

STEPHEN. Yes. Historic sites, sports teams, good seafood, *(pause)* crabs.

JIM. Don't get out much.

STEPHEN. I suppose your wife cooks.

JIM. I'm divorced.

STEPHEN. I'm sorry.

JIM. Not askin' for condolences.

STEPHEN. You have kids?

JIM. Two grown ones…gone their way.

STEPHEN I'm divorced too. Like yours, the kids have flown the coop…live in the burbs. *(Pause)* They hardly ever come in.

JIM. Come in to where?

STEPHEN. Philadelphia, where I got on. A condo in Rittenhouse Square.

JIM. Rittenhouse Square. Overheard from passengers, it's pretty fancy. Expect you'd live somewhere like that.

STEPHEN. Here you go again. Look, it's just a one-bedroom for little old me. *(Pause)* Well, it does have a big balcony with a view to the park.

JIM. You might guess where I live…

STEPHEN. Where?

JIM. In the Kresson neighborhood. You know the little perma-stone covered row houses with the stoops.

STEPHEN. I've heard about you Baltimoreans sitting out on them.

JIM. That's the deal.

STEPHEN. I'll bet you've got some friendly folk next door to keep you company... out there on those *(pause)* stooops.

JIM. Sure. If they haven't had an overdose.

STEPHEN. We've got some parts of town like that.

JIM. It didn't use to be that way. It was a nice place to bring up the kids. Now they've left, along with the wife... I guess I should go too, but where?

(Jim stares off into space.)

STEPHEN. There must be somewhere.

JIM. Maybe something in me just doesn't want to move. Stuck there. You know, not too far from the train station.

STEPHEN. You've been working on the railroad a long time?

JIM. Since I got out of high school. Done every job there is, up to conductor.

STEPHEN. Really?

JIM. Yeah. Those were the days. But then I guess they thought I was getting too old, so they shoved me back behind the cafe bar.

STEPHEN. So, you've been going up and down these tracks a while?

JIM. Yep, up and down.... You know, I thought I might do something else...maybe even be ...a "guy like you."

STEPHEN. That's something to think twice about.

JIM. Don't worry. It wasn't going to happen. My father talked me out of college. He was 'fraid I'd be a better man than him. That kind of stuff.

STEPHEN. That's a bummer.

JIM. Yeah, I was bitter for a long time, but I got over it.

STEPHEN. What about retirement?

JIM. Got three years to go…if I can last.

(Jim frowns and worriedly rubs his chest near his heart.)

STEPHEN. Three years isn't that long.

JIM. I'll try to hang on.

STEPHEN. I don't know why you put it that way.

JIM. Don't want to talk about it. So… what's your story?

STEPHEN. Me? Stephen Logan?

JIM. Righto, Mr. Logan.

STEPHEN. Mr. Byrnes, I don't know what to tell you.

JIM. I'll tell you what, I'm gonna step back behind the bar again while you think it over. *(Stands)*

STEPHEN. Oh, come on. Stay. I'll give it a shot.

JIM. *(Sits)* I'm listening…

STEPHEN. *(Takes a deep breath.)* Truth is, I didn't want to be an investment banker. It was my father's business; he wanted me to tag along. And hell, I did. Over the years it wrapped itself around me. Now look at me, Mr. Byrnes, the job and Stephen Logan have become one big glob.

JIM. That bad?

STEPHEN. At this point, it doesn't make any difference whether I like it or not. I just do it.

JIM. You sound stuck too.

STEPHEN. Something like that.

JIM. What would you've done different?

STEPHEN. Honestly…I wanted to be a pilot. I had a stint in the air force after college. Had some flight training. *(Pause)* Thought it would be an exciting life.

JIM. Funny. In that case, we both would'a been in the travel business.

STEPHEN. *(Chuckles)* Ha, I guess you could say that.

JIM. But you told me you like trains.

STEPHEN. I certainly do. Of course, depends where you're going.

JIM. True, you can't take a train to Dublin.

STEPHEN. Come on. That's ridiculous.

JIM. Not really, I have relatives living in Ireland.

STEPHEN. Then go see them, for God's sake.

JIM. Can't afford to.

STEPHEN. You're not that hard up.

JIM. You think on my pay, I could put away enough to take a trip like that?

STEPHEN. Sure, you can. You just don't want to.

JIM. Maybe I need the money for other stuff…told ya I've got kids.

STEPHEN. Uh-huh. That you did.

JIM. I could spend it on the trip, but something else would have to go…

STEPHEN. You should set priorities.

JIM. Priorities. I don't need to hear that! You live in another world. You don't know how guys like you piss me off.

STEPHEN. Mr. Byrnes, I thought we were finally getting friendly.

JIM. Friendly? See those tracks out there? You and me are on different sides of 'em. You might be stuck in your job, but look at the life you lead. Have you ever looked at the lives of "guys like me?"

STEPHEN. "Guys like you?" Mr. Byrnes, until we get to Essex Junction, you and I are on the same track.

JIM. Yeah, we'll just have to endure it.

STEPHEN. We might try changing the subject. *(Pause)* To one of mutual interest.

JIM. Mutual interest. Just what might that be?

STEPHEN. Women.

JIM. Women?

STEPHEN. That's right.

JIM. *(Laughing)* You really want me back at the bar, don't you?

STEPHEN. Haven't we both been on the marriage *track*?

(Jim stares at Stephen with a transfixed expression, as if curious.)

JIM. Yeh, but I don't wanna get back on now.

STEPHEN. We could trade stories about our *(pause)* former wives.

JIM. Give me a break.

STEPHEN. We could commiserate together. Come on, what else have we got to do?

JIM. *(With mixed feelings.)* Well, what the hell. Something to talk about. *(Pause)* So go ahead, tell me about that ex-wife of yours.

STEPHEN. You go first.

JIM. Well, you brought up the subject.

STEPHEN. True, I did...

JIM. Don't worry; you can't imagine the personal stuff I hear on this job. People on trains open up like they never would off the rails.

STEPHEN. That could be. In any case, I'll go on. *(Pause)* Oh, yes, the wife... Catherine. She was the academic kind, ambitious in that little world. Very independent. Always going to conferences in her linguistics field. Hobnobbing with professors.

JIM. Don't mean much to me.

STEPHEN. It's funny... With all her damn linguistics, she didn't have much to say to me. *(Softly)* I guess she didn't consider me the intellectual type, didn't care for my business world.

JIM. Guess she wouldn't like me.

STEPHEN. Who knows? Anyway, she finally decided she didn't like me, and just flew off.

JIM. With what I reckon was a bundle of your money.

STEPHEN. Not a penny. She inherited a fortune from her dad.

JIM. Ohhh. Another one.

STEPHEN. That she is. Only this time, I don't mind your saying it. I'm glad she has her own money. At least I am free of her.

JIM. *(Hesitantly)* That's not the way I felt about my wife.

STEPHEN. What do you mean?

JIM. I wanted my wife to stay.

STEPHEN. She left you too?

JIM. Yeah, she did... Jane was a wild one. Just like a gypsy. You should have seen her all dressed up in crazy skirts and beads.

STEPHEN. I'd never have guessed you'd have a wife like that.

JIM. Can't figure it myself... She found a guy, probably like her. *(Pause)* Never met him. But sure enough, they ran off together. Stranded me with the kids.

STEPHEN. Must have been hard on you.

JIM. Well, the kids were on their way out, anyway.

STEPHEN. Do you ever hear from her?

JIM. Not much. *(Pause)* Stephen, I still love the gal...

STEPHEN. *(Startled)* From what you tell me, that's a wonder.

JIM. Maybe she gave me something. Something I ain't got. Damed if I know. Anyhow, it's been five years without her. Five long years.

STEPHEN. Gone on any dates?

JIM. Not a one.

STEPHEN. I can understand.

JIM. How bout you?

STEPHEN. Pretty much the same.

(After a pause, Stephen hesitantly begins speaking.)

STEPHEN. Well, there was Stephanie, didn't last long...

JIM. How's that?

STEPHEN. Stephanie, she was alright. Can't blame her. It was me. *(Pause)* You can't say I'm a happy guy, but to be honest, I really don't want to change.

JIM. So here we are, two miserable guys.

STEPHEN. Probably our own damn faults.

JIM. Wouldn't know how to make it right. *(Pause)*

STEPHEN. Well, we sure aren't going to figure it out now, so let's drop it for the rest of the trip.

JIM. I'll go along with that.

STEPHEN. Can we shake on it? (*Stephen extends his hand*)

JIM. Well...

>(*A pause, then Jim backs off, and with hesitation, reaches for and shakes Stephen's hand.*)

STEPHEN. There you go, Mr. Brynes.

JIM. Call me Jim.

STEPHEN. Will do, Jim. Listen, I didn't sleep well last night. Worried about catching this early train. If you don't mind, I'll just take a little snooze.

JIM. Go ahead, Stephen. I wish I could too, but maybe a customer will come on.

>(*Stephen leans back in his seat and closes his eyes. Music begins to play.*)

LIGHTS FADE

SCENE TWO

(AT RISE. Lights come up on the same train car, about an hour later.)

ANNOUNCER. *(Voice Over)* Now arriving at Stamford Station.

STEPHEN. Oh, my goodness. That was a nice little nap... *(Yawns)* Say, where are we?

JIM. You slept straight through our stop in New York. We just pulled into Stamford, Connecticut.

STEPHEN. New England, getting closer...

(Jim heads back to the bar. The train stops and JENNIFER, a well-dressed, middle-aged woman, comes into the cafe car and sits down across from Stephen. She looks straight ahead and pays no attention to him. Finally, Stephen turns to her and speaks.)

STEPHEN. Good morning.

JENNIFER. It's 12:30 in the afternoon.

(Another moment of silence.)

STEPHEN. Nice day, isn't it?

JENNIFER. *(Looks out the window.)* So it seems.

STEPHEN. I am on my way to Vermont. How about you?

JENNIFER. Northampton...Massachusetts.

STEPHEN. Northampton. That's where Smith College is. My sister went to Smith some years back.

JENNIFER. I'm going to the college too. But if you would, please excuse me. I need my coffee.

(Jennifer gets up and goes to the bar.)

STEPHEN. *(Under his breath)* Hope she has better luck then I had.

JENNIFER. *(To Jim)* May I please have a cup of coffee?

JIM. Yes, ma'am. You can find the cream and sugar on the counter.

JENNIFER. Oh.

(Jennifer hands Jim some money.)

JIM. Your change, ma'am.

JENNIFER. Why don't you keep it?

JIM. Well, thank you.

JENNIFER. You're welcome.

(Moves to the counter for the cream and sugar.)

JIM. *(To himself)* Nice lady. Not many so generous.

JENNIFER. Please, sir, would you tell me how long it might be to Northampton?

JIM. Oh 'bout an hour-and-a-half.

JENNIFER. So I'll have time to finish my book. Hopefully, that man across from me will allow me to do so.

(Jennifer heads back to her seat. She sits down and buries her nose in her book. Stephen looks at her with a blank stare, not knowing what to say. Finally, he ventures a few words.)

STEPHEN. Um, I don't mean to be intrusive, Ms., but I was wondering what you'll be doing at Smith?

JENNIFER. You don't give up, do you?

STEPHEN. I didn't mean to bother you.

JENNIFER. If you must know, I have been appointed the Dean of Libraries.

STEPHEN. Quite an honor.

JENNIFER. Indeed. It's the position I've been aiming for, since way back.

STEPHEN. As they say, you have arrived.

JENNIFER. It's a wonder I did.

STEPHEN. How is that?

JENNIFER. Now listen, and keep in mind, I am not going to say anything more. *(Pause)* My mother was a famous actress and tried to push me into the theater. Believe me, I did work at it: acting lessons, play tryouts, *(Pause)* bit parts... It didn't take long to find out the stage wasn't for me. I am sure you noticed, I'm the bookish sort, so off I went to library school. Oh, did my mother hold it against me.

STEPHEN. You had the guts to oppose your mother... I couldn't with my father.

JENNIFER. Please, if you don't mind, I just want to sit quietly and read.

STEPHEN. Well I'm glad to see someone reading these days. Not that I do much myself.

JENNIFER. *(Jennifer hesitates, sighs, and exclaims.)* I am glad to hear you think that way. One wonders if today's students will ever take a book out again. Libraries are my life, but I worry they may all disappear.

STEPHEN. That is worrisome.

JENNIFER. *(Exasperated)* Sir, are we now finished this conversation?

(Stephen backs off, picks up the magazine and thumbs through it in silence. The train rumbles on. Music is heard. Jennifer goes back to reading her book. Jim walks over to Stephen.)

JIM. Say, Stephen, it's lunch time. Want anything?

STEPHEN.   Wow, the service has sure improved since this morning.

JIM.   *(Laughing)* Take it while you can.

STEPHEN.   How about one of your ham and cheese sandwiches. And a beer?

JIM.   *(Light heartedly)* A beer? Stephen, I am surprised. I thought a guy like you would want wine.

STEPHEN.   *(Jokingly)* Guys like me have all kinds of tastes.

JIM.   Alright. Want the sandwich warmed up?

STEPHEN.   Sure, why not?

JIM.   *(To Jennifer)* Anything for you, ma'am?

JENNIFER.   No, thank you.

JIM.   As you wish.

> *(Jim returns to the bar. Stephen sits back in his seat and closes his eyes as if napping. Music is heard. Jim brings Stephen his sandwich and beer.)*

JIM.   Here you go, Stephen.

STEPHEN.   Much obliged.

JIM.   My pleasure, sir.

> *(Stephen munches on his sandwich with pleasure and sipping his beer, with an occasional glance at Jennifer.)*

STEPHEN.   *(To Jennifer, shyly)* Might I ask what you are reading?

JENNIFER.   It's a novel by Elizabeth Bowen. One of my preferred authors. I don't know that you would be interested. You said yourself, you don't read much.

JIM.   He reads the stock page.

JENNIFER.   Ah ha. *(With glee)* I had a notion he's from Wall Street.

JIM. He is, but there's more to the guy than that. You should get to know him.

STEPHEN. *(To Jennifer)* It's just a job I fell into…or should I say, got pushed into. Never attained the heights you have.

JENNIFER. Still, you're making the big bucks.

STEPHEN. I do okay.

JENNIFER. The way I look at it, Wall Street is the ruination of this country. So much money moving around; yet it produces nothing of value.

STEPHEN. Yeah, you liberals from academia forget who manages the college endowments that pay for your cushy jobs.

JENNIFER. Actually…I hadn't thought of that. Still doesn't change my mind about *(pause)* Wall Street.

STEPHEN. I'm not asking you to.

JENNIFER. And I won't.

STEPHEN. Can I tell you something that might interest you?

JENNIFER. *(Facetiously)* I'm listening.

STEPHEN. True, I'm not the literary type, I don't know who Elizabeth Bowen is, but I do like art. Believe it or not, I have a little collection of my own.

JENNIFER. I imagine you can afford it.

STEPHEN. Don't think I'm in the one percent.

JENNIFER. *(Coyly.)* Well maybe the two percent.

STEPHEN. Oh, come on.

JENNIFER. However much you have, I hope you spend it well.

STEPHEN. I try. But let me tell you, there's a painting in your Smith College Art Museum that is one of my favorites. Of course, I couldn't afford it, even if they were willing to sell. Maybe when you get there, you might take a look.

JENNIFER. Which painting is that?

STEPHEN. It's by the French painter, Camille Corot. Do you know him?

JENNIFER. Of course, he's a famous artist.

STEPHEN. It's a portrait of a woman. She gazes mysteriously out into space. I keep a picture of it on my iPhone.

(Pulls out his iPhone and shows her.)

JENNIFER. She's lovely.

STEPHEN. Well, she's no Mona Lisa, but there is something about her expression that makes you wonder what she's thinking.

JIM. Who knows what any gal is thinking?

(Jennifer scowls at Jim.)

STEPHEN. Do we ever know what anyone is thinking?

JENNIFER. So perhaps there is another side to you. A more thoughtful side you hide away. But that's true of most people.

STEPHEN. So that would mean you have another side too. I bet somewhere, tucked away inside, there must be a 'bank of charm.'

JENNIFER. *(Coyly)* Wouldn't you know it, he comes up with a money metaphor… 'bank of charm.,' huh?

JIM. Sure, with that charm, I'll bet she's got a booming love life.

STEPHEN. Jim, I think you are on to something…

JENNIFER. *(With an air of flamboyance.)* Can't you guys imagine that I put my 'bank of charm' to good use?

JIM. No doubt.

JENNIFER. I do have my admirers. You can rest assured, I haven't been neglected.

STEPHEN. You're speaking of love. That's a big arena. You know men do fall in love.

JIM. *(pointing to himself.)* True, *this* man fell in love.

STEPHEN. Yeah, and I've heard it said that every man has an image of an ideal woman stamped inside... Maybe that's why I like keeping Corot's painting on my iPhone.

JENNIFER. So, you appreciate both art and psychology? Rather unusual for a man in your world.

STEPHEN. Unusual? Is that bad?

JENNIFER. Not at all. *(Pause)* It adds color, like you see in that painting you admire.

STEPHEN. Honestly, I don't read psychology. As I said, it's just something I've heard.

JENNIFER. The idea seems to have stuck with you...

STEPHEN. It has. Take a look at the painting, and maybe you'll understand why.

JENNIFER. Trust I shall visit the museum...when I have the time.

STEPHEN. But how can I hear what you thought of it? I'll probably never see you again.

JENNIFER. *(With a laugh, Jennifer reaches out and touches Stephen's hand)* Should I be distressed?

STEPHEN. *(With a smile.)* Try not to be.

JENNIFER. Well, I'll do my best.

STEPHEN. You know, Miss, there's someone I see in you.

JENNIFER. *(Coyly)* Ah ha, maybe that someone matches your image of the ideal woman. Who might she be? Does she look like the comely lady in the painting? I'll take a look in the bathroom mirror to see who you are talking about.

(Playfully, pointing to the restroom.)

STEPHEN. Well, please report back.

JENNIFER. Oh, I will.

(Jennifer gets up and walks towards the restroom, Stage Right. She turns, looks back at Stephen with a wink, then exits, gently closing its door behind her.)

JIM. There's that 'bank of charm.' I knew it was there!

(Stephen grins at Jim, leans back in his seat and closes his eyes. Music is heard.)

LIGHTS FADE

SCENE THREE

(AT RISE. Music fades as the Stage Lights come up on the same train car, later that day. Jim is again behind the bar, while Jennifer is back sitting again across from Stephen. Their mood has changed, and it is clear that they now enjoy one another's company.)

ANNOUNCER. *(Voice Over)* Springfield Station. Please ensure you have all your personal belongings, and watch your step.

(AGNES 38, enters with a flourish. She is dressed like a refugee from the Hippie era, flowing paisley skirt, gauze blouse and strings of multi-colored beads.)

AGNES. Well, hello everyone! Looks like a comfy little bunch here. Didn't they use to call these 'club cars?'

(Jennifer regards Agnes with a scowl, but says nothing.)

JIM. Welcome aboard, ma'am...And yes, we've gotten quite 'clubby' here.

STEPHEN. *(Dryly)* Hello.

(Still standing, Agnes turns to Stephen and fixes her gaze on him.)

AGNES. I have the strange feeling you've been in my life *(pause)* in the past.

STEPHEN. I doubt that.

AGNES. *(Mysteriously)* Seriously, like in another time....another place.

STEPHEN. Ms., I think you must be imagining it.

AGNES. Maybe. It's that you have the aura of someone I've been with.

STEPHEN. *(Annoyed)* Let's leave it at that.

(Stephen turns from Agnes and opens the magazine. Agnes looks disappointed and turns to Jennifer.)

AGNES. You seem the silent sort, lady.

JENNIFER. Let's say, 'reserved.'

AGNES. Reserved. Got it. Mind if I sit here?

(Agnes points to the seat behind Stephen.)

STEPHEN. *(Hesitantly)* I guess not.

(Agnes twirls into her seat, as if in a dance.)

AGNES. *(To Stephen)* Seems the silent lady is not interested in conversation…Maybe you and I can talk. I'll bet we'll har-mon-ize.

(Jennifer looks over and rolls her eyes.)

STEPHEN. *(Coughs)* Don't know about that.

AGNES. Can't we give it a chance?

(Stephen raises his magazine and slides further into the booth, away from Agnes. Jim has been watching this whole interchange, and says from the bar.)

JIM. Ma'am, you want anything?

(Agnes gets up and crosses to the bar.)

AGNES. A white wine.

JIM. Now here's a lady with class.

AGNES. Well, thanks, kind sir.

JIM. That'll be four-fifty.

AGNES. Oh, four-fifty, huh? Need to search my purse for it. Can I pay you later?

(Jim nods, then chuckles to himself. Agnes crosses to her seat and takes a long gulp of wine, accidently spilling a little on Stephen's pant leg. Jennifer abruptly pulls away from Agnes to avoid the spilled wine.)

STEPHEN. Can't you be more careful?

AGNES. Uh…sorry.

(She tries to wipe his thigh with a napkin, but he shoos her away. She returns to her seat, embarrassed. Jim notices her discomfort and brings her a fresh glass of wine.)

JIM. Here you go, ma'am. On the house.

AGNES. Thanks.

JIM. My pleasure. Tell me, where're you getting off?

AGNES. Montpelier. I've got friends picking me up to drive to a session in the woods. Near Stowe.

JIM. A session?

AGNES. A real groovy session… you know, uh, consciousness expanding.

JENNIFER. *(Under her breath)* I can see the need.

AGNES. Oh, the silent lady has a comment.

JENNIFER. There won't be another word.

AGNES. Cool.

STEPHEN. Ms.…?

AGNES. Agnes.

STEPHEN. Agnes…this fine lady and I have gotten to know each other. We've been riding for a while. There have been some nice moments, so maybe…

AGNES. What are you trying to say?

STEPHEN. Not to be impolite, but maybe you could leave the lady…

JIM. Agnes, Stephen's right 'bout that. But I'll tell you what; you can come talk with me at the bar, if you like. It gets pretty lonesome here.

AGNES. *(Agnes looks at Jim.)* Oh, so his name is Stephen? If you don't mind, I'll be more comfortable just sitting where I am. Maybe I'll come get some more wine later.

> *(Music is heard. Everyone sits back in silence while Jennifer returns to her book. The sound of the train rumbles and fades.)*

AGNES. Stephen, won't you venture a few words?

STEPHEN. *(Annoyed)* Must I?

AGNES. *(Sweetly)* That would please me.

STEPHEN. Well, I am curious. What's that session in the woods all about? What do you mean, 'consciousness expanding?'

> *(Jennifer buries her nose in her book, pretending not to hear.)*

AGNES. We all try to find the best in each other…then soar with it… *(Gestures)* Upwards. You should try it.

> *(Jennifer rolls her eyes again.)*

STEPHEN. Hmm…me soar? *(Under his breath)* I did want to, in my own way.

AGNES. You want to come along?

STEPHEN. Unh… no thanks. That wasn't in my plans.

AGNES. You would fit right in.

STEPHEN. Unlikely.

AGNES. Well…maybe another time.

STEPHEN. Say, Montpelier, isn't that the capital of Vermont, where all those damn communist politicians hang out? Guys like, Bernie Sanders?

JENNIFER. Correction; Sanders lives in Burlington, when he's not in Washington.

AGNES. I can't believe it! The silent lady speaks again.

JIM. Seems she knows her politicians.

JENNIFER. I know that much. And I like Bernie. He's got some good ideas about equality. *(Looking at Stephen with a mischievous smile.)* Ideas that might upset you Wall Street guys.

STEPHEN. I'm on my way to vacation, and I don't need to get upset.

AGNES. You folks should know, I'm not really into politicians. I don't know one from the other. I just want, peace and love...and they're not giving me either.

STEPHEN. Hmmm. Peace and love...huh.

JIM. I'll settle for just a bit of peace before Northampton. Shouldn't be long now.

(Music is heard. Train whistle. A pause, then...)

ANNOUNCER. *(Voice Over)* Northampton Station. Please ensure you have all your personal belongings and watch the gap between the train and the platform as you exit.

JENNIFER. Well, this is my stop.

(Stephen and Agnes look over at Jennifer. Jennifer silently gets up and gathers her things, as the train comes to a stop.)

AGNES. Goodbye, silent lady!

(Jennifer scowls at Agnes, then turns to Stephen.)

STEPHEN. Don't forget to look at that painting.

JENNIFER. Don't worry, I won't forget. It was…a pleasure talking to you.

(Jennifer shakes Stephen's hand and points to Agnes.)

JENNIFER. …and good luck with *this* one… *(Agnes scowls at Jennifer who turns to Jim.)* And sir, best wishes to you.

JIM. Likewise. And Ms., thanks for your generosity back at the bar.

(Jennifer nods, takes one last look at Stephen, and then exits.)

ANNOUNCER. *(Voice Over)* Now leaving Northampton Station.

(Train whistles. Stephen and Agnes sit back in silence as the Music rises.)

LIGHTS FADE

SCENE FOUR

(AT RISE. Moments later, lights come up on the Cafe Car. Music fades. Jim still putters behind the bar, as Agnes turns to Stephen.)

AGNES. Well, Stephen, it's just you and me now...

(Stephen looks at Agnes with an alarmed expression.)

JIM. Hey!

AGNES. Oh, sorry, Jim.

JIM. It's ok. Nothing new.

STEPHEN. Jim, we've all been there.

JIM. Unfortunately. How about another beer, Stephen?

STEPHEN. Why not?

(Jim brings the beer over to Stephen's table.)

STEPHEN. Thanks pal.

(Jim takes Stephen's empty bottle and returns to the bar. Stephen sips at his beer and gazes out into space in a more relaxed mood.)

AGNES. Say, Stephen, mind if I come over and join you?

STEPHEN. What's wrong with the way it is?

AGNES. Hard talking to you from back here.

STEPHEN. We're perfect strangers.

AGNES No, like I said, I have known you in the past.

STEPHEN. But you haven't.

AGNES. Stephen, I am a wanderer… always roaming about, ever since leaving the orphanage.

STEPHEN. Ohhh, an orphan. We've all complained about our parents, but you have none to complain about.

AGNES. True. No mother. No father. But there have been lots of people along the way, *(pause)* and yes, including you. Still I feel lonely.

JIM. *(glumly)* Agnes, I can understand.

AGNES. Stephen, coming across a guy like you, I get a special feeling. Please, it would make me real happy if I could sit down with you.

STEPHEN. *(Hesitantly)* …all right, come on around.

(Agnes gets up, and with one of her funny little dances, sits beside Stephen.)

AGNES. Stephen, maybe it's wrong to ask, but are you married?

STEPHEN. That's really none of your business.

AGNES. I'll bet you are… a good-looking guy like you.

(Jim looks over at the two in dismay.)

STEPHEN. I don't need flattery.

AGNES. It's not that. I really mean it.

(Stephen turns his head with displeasure showing his lack of interest in the conversation. Jim continues to look unhappy.)

STEPHEN. Can't we talk about something else?

AGNES. Sure. What's with that painting you were talking about with the…silent lady?

STEPHEN. That's something personal between me and her.

AGNES. Sorry, then I guess I'll just talk about little old me.

STEPHEN. Oh, wait a minute.

AGNES. Don't worry. Nothing too outrageous.

(Agnes lays her hand on Stephen's shoulder. Stephen stares at her for a moment and gently takes her hand away and turns to look out the window again.)

AGNES. Listen Stephen, I was on top of Macchu Pichu last month. In Peru. It blew my mind away. The light, the air. It was really a high.

JIM. Maybe she was smokin' something.

(Agnes smiles at Jim.)

STEPHEN. They say people get dizzy up there.

AGNES. Not me. Not for a minute.

JIM. Oh boy.

AGNES. Stephen, I met a woman on the plateau… Bethany. No, it's nothing like you might imagine, but we did become friends. Close.

JIM. It's gettin' serious.

AGNES. It was serious. We had a lot of long talks. Talked about everything. Bethany told me things I didn't realize…about myself.

JIM. What sorts of things?

STEPHEN. Do we really need to know?

AGNES. I want you to. *(Agnes puts her hand again on Stephen's shoulder.)* She said I have a rare gift.

(Stephen quickly removes her hand from his shoulder now with increasing annoyance.)

STEPHEN. A rare gift? What might that be?

AGNES. Bethany said I am…prescient *(She pronounces it 'press-scent.')*

JIM. What for God's sake is press-scent?

AGNES. It means I can sense the future.

STEPHEN. The word is pronounced presh-shee-ent.

JIM. Tell us about that future stuff.

AGNES. Look at my friend Stephen here. I sense that we could have a future together.

STEPHEN. You've got to be out of your mind.

JIM. That she is, but you know with it all, I kinda like the gal. She reminds me of someone I used to know...

AGNES. That's cr-ryp-tic, Jim. I'll guess she was someone you liked.

JIM. I did, but she left me.

AGNES. That's so sad...I know you will find someone else.

JIM. It sounds like you are saying that, for you, there's no future, with a guy like me.

AGNES. Don't take it to heart, Jim. It's just that Stephen is more...

STEPHEN. You can forget that.

AGNES. Why is it the men I want, never want me?

STEPHEN. Maybe there is someone else out there for you, but, you are right, it is not me.

AGNES. Don't worry Stephen, I may glimpse the future, but I can't move there. Once I get off this train, we will never see each other again.

JIM. Sounds like she's stuck too, Stephen. Just like us.

AGNES. Right. Stuck in the past.

JIM. The past?

AGNES. I have a husband.

JIM. Where's the lucky fellow? *(Under his breath.)* Well, maybe not so lucky...

AGNES. I left him for another man. A guy like Stephen...and then he left me.

JIM. What about your husband?

AGNES. What about him?

JIM. Maybe he wants you back.

AGNES. He just vanished.

JIM. Never heard from him?

AGNES. Never. *(Pause)* Left me in limbo.

(Jim opens his mouth as if to speak, but Agnes stops him)

AGNES. It's okay Jim. You don't have to say anything. You know, Bethany told me something else. She said, "Courage woman. Stick with it. Something good will happen you can't imagine." Well, I hope so. But here I am now on this damn train...alone.

JIM. Agnes, how about another wine? Maybe it'll help you feel better. *(Pause)* Don't worry, I'll take care of it. *(with a wink and under his breath)* Or Amtrak will.

STEPHEN. Now Jim, don't get yourself in trouble.

JIM. If they fire me, what's the difference?

STEPHEN. Why would you say that?

AGNES. Maybe it's something he doesn't want to talk about. Something *personal*, for him.

JIM. Agnes, I 'preciate you saying that.

AGNES. I try to be considerate. You know I was hoping Stephen here, would buy me the wine...but thanks, Jim.

(Becoming tipsy, Agnes dejectedly walks over to the bar to get the wine and returns to her seat.)

JIM. Agnes, we'll be arriving in Montepelier in a few minutes.

AGNES. Alright. I'll just sit here 'til then and sip my wine.

JIM. I'll miss ya.

(Agnes holds her wine glass up as if to make a toast smiling at it glowingly, then turns to Jim.)

AGNES. Nice of you to say.

JIM. It's gonna be a dull ride after Montepelier.

STEPHEN. I'm ready for that.

(Moments pass, silence, the train whistle is heard. Finally, Jim realizing Agnes is becoming inebriated says…)

JIM. Say, Agnes, how 'bout a quick coffee before you step off.

(Stephen turns the other way and looks out the window.)

AGNES. Want me to come to the bar?

JIM. No, I'll bring it over, with some cream and sugar, just in case.

(Smiling, Jim brings the coffee over to Agnes who is still sipping her wine. Ignoring Jim and Agnes, Stephen continues looking out the window.)

AGNES. Thanks. You're a real generous guy. *(Clearly avoiding the coffee, Agnes refuses to put her wine glass down and finally offers a toast.)* I really wish you all the best, Jim. *(Jim stares at Agnes, then returns to the bar. Agnes finishes her wine, waving the glass with a sad motion and whispers, sadly.)* …here's to you…

(Stephen continues looking out the window in silence. Music is heard. The train rolls on.)

ANNOUNCER. *(Voice Over)* Now approaching Montpelier Station.

JIM. Agnes, you will be leaving the train soon.

AGNES. *(To Stephen)* …Stephen, maybe if I didn't have to get off… things could be different…

STEPHEN. Dammit, that's it. I'm going to take a turn at the bar.

(Stephen gets up and maneuvers awkwardly around seated Agnes and joins Jim at the bar.)

AGNES. *(Sadly)* Guess I better get my things together…

JIM. Can I give you a hand?

AGNES. No I'll manage, Jim.

(Agnes gets up and returns to her original seat behind Stephen, gathers her things together, and takes a few steps toward the bar. She is even more feeling the effects of the wine and walks with a bit of a stagger. Suddenly, she stops in front of the bar.)

AGNES. *(Tipsy, but emphatic, turning to Jim.)* Jim. I know you like me, for whatever insane reason. But, forget it, please. *(Turns to Stephen.)* And you Stephen…that silent lady friend of yours…she wouldn't even give me the time of day. Who the hell does she think she is?

(Stephen throws his arms up in the air and shrugs. Stephen stands and crosses downstage. Agnes follows and stands in front of him confrontationally.)

AGNES. And you are just like her. She's stuck on her own rock and won't move off. And you won't either. I'm standing right in front of you, and you don't even see me. You don't have the slightest idea who I am, and don't understand anything. You never will. I can only pity you.

STEPHEN. Don't.

AGNES. Oh yes, I'm off to that session in the woods. I've been to so many. Despite what I said, that stuff really doesn't do it for me.

I always come away, empty. Oh, God, maybe I can find Bethany somewhere. She'll help me. *(Tears in her eyes.)* ... I wish I could ride this train on forever... on and on, to some beautiful place where everyone loves me...

(Agnes begins to weep. After a moment, Jim steps from behind the bar and approaches her.)

JIM. Agnes, I'm sorry, so sorry...

ANNOUNCER. *(Voice Over)* Montpelier Station. Please ensure you have all your personal belongings, and please watch your step.

(Agnes nods her head sadly and walks to the exit door beyond the restroom. Jim follows her to the door, opens it for her, and then very slowly closes the door behind her. Music rises as the train whistle blows.)

LIGHTS FADE

SCENE FIVE

(Soon after Agnes departs, Stephen returns to his seat. Jim returns to the bar polishing glasses. Finally Jim speaks.)

JIM. Don't make me feel good, a woman crying like that.

STEPHEN. I know what you mean, Jim. But what could we have done?

JIM. Beats me. She's like one of those kids from the Sixties. Thought they had all gone.

STEPHEN. Seems they haven't.

JIM. Her friend, Bethany, what's all that about?

STEPHEN. For all we know, Bethany doesn't even exist; just someone in Agnes' mind she looks to.

JIM. Don't know what you mean.

STEPHEN. She's searching.

JIM. For what?

STEPHEN. We'll never know.

JIM. That librarian thinks she's found it all. *(Pause)* Someday, she'll realize she hasn't.

STEPHEN. That's something we can't tell her.

JIM. Even if we could, would she listen?

STEPHEN. Jim, look, in all fairness, I have to say the librarian has her gifts.

JIM. Hah, I see you've got a thing with that gal.

STEPHEN. I won't deny that.

JIM. But, Steve, you're right. Just like us men, the gals have their bad points, and their good points.

STEPHEN. Jim, could I have been blind to Agnes in that way? (*Stephen gazes off into space.*)

JIM. Ah, Agnes...I wanted to wrap my arms around her and kiss her.

STEPHEN. Like me with the librarian. You can't get Agnes, and that crazy ex-wife of yours out of your head, can you?

JIM. I just can't.

STEPHEN. I understand, Jim. My ex-wife Catherine's memory still stirs in these brain cells. (*Points to his head.*)

JIM. Stephen, you know there's been some strange runs, but none like this one. (*Pause*) Coming on the train, those two gals sure gave us a spin.

STEPHEN. A spin? I thought I was just going to Vermont, not a trip to the tacky past.

JIM. (*with a laugh*) Well, maybe you got on the wrong train...

STEPHEN. Still, Jim, on another train, I would never have met those two.

JIM. That's a point.

STEPHEN. Like people you meet along the way, maybe they had a message.

JIM. What could it have been?

STEPHEN. I'd tell you had I bothered to listen.

JIM. Now it's too late.

STEPHEN. Jim, I never even got the librarian's name...

JIM. You didn't ask her?

STEPHEN. Now they both are gone. (*Stephen looks out into space wistfully.*) So very gone...

JIM. Like any passengers, leaving the train...

STEPHEN. You've seen them come and go.

JIM. That I have. *(Pause)* But Stephen, I do wonder if your librarian friend will go see the painting.

STEPHEN. Guess we'll never know, and it may not mean anything to her. That painting. The damn thing haunts me. Like I said, there is a picture of a perfect woman stuck inside us. *(pause)* Ahhh, and when we find her, she turns out to be a hell of a lot of trouble.

(*Jim and Stephen remain silent for a while as music plays.*)

JIM. Say, Stephen, it's still a while 'til Essex Junction. How about a little card game to pass the time? We can talk over a hand of gin rummy.

STEPHEN. Why not?

JIM. Beats solitaire.

(*Jim returns to the booth from the bar and sits opposite Stephen. Jim pulls out a pack of cards and deals a hand.*)

STEPHEN. Tell me, Jim. I'll be going to see my friend in St. Johnsbury. What are you going to do?

JIM. From Essex Junction where you get off, we go on to St. Albans, a few minutes up the tracks. The end of the run. They put me up in a crummy hotel, and then back I go, day after tomorrow, on the early-morning train.

STEPHEN. Back to Baltimore?

JIM. Back to Baltimore... You know Stephen, it's eight o'clock, almost dark. It's been 'bout ten hours since you got on the train this morning.

STEPHEN. Ten hours...

JIM. And all the while, you and I, we've come a distance.

STEPHEN. I am not sure what you mean...?

JIM. You know...

STEPHEN. A little closer? I guess that's what you're trying to say. The way it started out, getting that coffee, I wouldn't have imagined.

JIM. Me neither.

STEPHEN. It's funny. This turned into one of those buddy road trip movies. But on a train.

(Jim looks at Stephen with a puzzled expression and rests his cards on the table. He pauses reflectively for a moment.)

JIM. You know, that talk about money stuff. Sorry 'bout what I said.

STEPHEN. Ah. Hell...Forget it, Jim. True, I was put off at the beginning, by your 'guys like you' talk. But I admit I have my own prejudices. I really don't have much to do with guys like you. To tell you the truth, I don't know much about them. And maybe I haven't had a high regard for them in the past. But I tried to keep my mouth shut.

JIM. I thought maybe you felt that way. Why wouldn't you?

STEPHEN. But it turns out we have lots we share. Tough fathers...never had the careers we wanted... divorced...

JIM. Living alone.

STEPHEN. More than anything, we've just enjoyed keeping company. *(Drops his cards.)* Gin. Deal me another hand.

JIM. Stephen, there's something else on my mind... I want to explain 'bout that coffee.

STEPHEN. It's okay. I had practically forgotten about it.

JIM. 'Preciate that. Still, let me tell you anyway.

STEPHEN. Alright…go on.

> *(They both lay their cards down on the table and stop playing. Jim wearily stands up from the table and looks down at Stephen.)*

JIM. I…I'm not well.

STEPHEN. What's wrong, Jim?

JIM. You know that thing with sugar in the blood?

STEPHEN. High?

JIM. Yeah. It's real high.

STEPHEN. There's medicine for that.

JIM. I have it. *(Pause)* The doctors tell me I should eat something right away, after I take my pills…that's why I didn't want to get up to serve you coffee. In my mind, I had to sit there and hack away on that sandwich.

STEPHEN. Now I understand.

JIM. But I guess I did overdo it a bit. Being sick can make you cranky.

STEPHEN. I'd probably be the same.

JIM. Naw… I was just being damn stubborn. Coulda gotten up for your coffee.

STEPHEN. Maybe on our next trip.

JIM. Not sure there will be one.

STEPHEN. Oh, stop that kind of talk.

JIM. Stephen. *(Pause)* My heart. Ain't good either.

> *(Stephen stands up and puts his hand on Jim's shoulder.)*

STEPHEN. Jim…

JIM. They tell me I'm on the edge. I know I am just telling you now…after all these hours.

STEPHEN. I am so glad you did.

JIM. Thought we were at a point, when I could.

STEPHEN. We are, Jim.

JIM. Steve, you were right about that trip to Dublin. I'm gonna make it, a priority. Gives me something to look forward to.

> *(Pause, the sound of the train whistle is heard. Jim takes Stephen's hand away, leans over the table and packs up the cards.)*

JIM. Stephen, anything else I can get you?

STEPHEN. *(Glumly)* Ahh, no thanks, Jim, I'll just ride it out.

> *(Jim heads back to the bar. Stephen sits quietly at his booth staring out the window. Sad music rises. The train whistles again.)*

JIM. Steve, comin' up to Essex Junction in 'bout three minutes.

STEPHEN. Three minutes? That's not much time left to us, after riding together for ten hours. That makes me real sad. *(Pause, Jim nods his head, Stephen stands up and paces around in silence, turns to Jim and says.)* Jim, would you give me your, *(pause)* uh, phone number?

JIM. Don't talk much on the phone, don't really have anybody to talk to. *(scrawls it on a paper bar napkin, hesitates)* But here it is.

STEPHEN. I'm going to call you when I get back.

JIM. That's a call I'm gonna take.

STEPHEN. Jim, please, let's not let it be the last one…

> *(Pause. Train music. Train whistle heard.)*

ANNOUNCER. *(Voice Over)* Essex Junction. Please ensure you have all your personal belongings and watch your step.

> *(Stephen gets up, gathers his things, and heads for the door. Jim follows him. They stand silently at the door for a moment together.*

Stephen nods to Jim. Jim briefly embraces Stephen. Stephen turns around and quickly exits the train. The train moves on. Jim very slowly returns to the bar and busies himself straightening up the countertop. He stops, stares blankly into space for a few seconds. LIGHTS DIM, until a single light shines on Jim, then slowly FADES OUT.)

CURTAIN

Train To Essex Junction was first performed at the Highview Arts Center in Louisville, Kentucky March, 2023.

ORIGINAL CAST

Jim Byrnes	John Heffley
Steven Logan	Beau Solley
Jennifer	Rayann Houghlin Walker
Agnes	Shannon Corbett
Announcer	Victor Hardly

Produced by	*Cambridge Concepts, LLC*

Director	Vin Morreale, Jr.
Stage Manager	Janice Walter
Lighting Designer	Taylor Torsky
Set Design	Jill Marie Schierbaum

This premiere production was nominated for a 2023 BEST NEW PLAY award by Arts Louisville.

TRAIN TO ESSEX JUNCTION 43

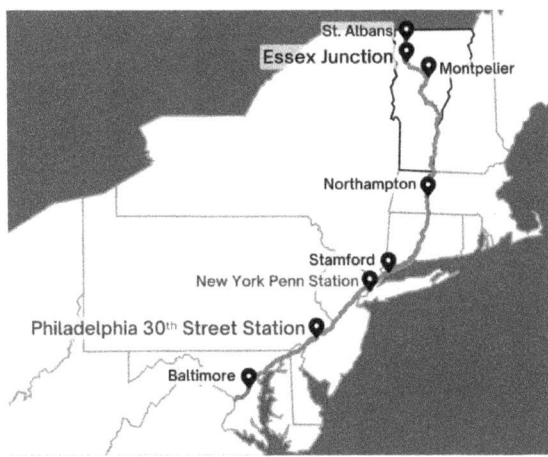

Map showing route of train to
Essex Junction, Vermont

Painting by Camille Corot at Smith College Art Museum
As referenced in the play

About The Playwright

David S. Traub, Jr. is a Philadelphia-based architect, author, and playwright.

Traub's first two plays, *Lincoln in Louisville* and *Woodford Place*, were inspired by his life growing up in his birthplace, Louisville, Kentucky. Both plays were produced and performed in that city. Traub attended university in Philadelphia, and stayed on there where he followed a career in architecture, all the while writing across a spectrum of genres.

In contrast to Louisville, where train travel is virtually non-existent, living on the East Coast allowed Traub to experience rail travel on the Amtrak trains which ply the tracks up and down the coastline, and up to New England as far as Vermont. *Train to Essex Junction*, therefore, has no roots thematically in his former life in Louisville. This new play is based upon an actual event in Traub's life traveling from Philadelphia to Vermont to visit friends.

As in his first two plays, a major theme of *Train to Essex Junction* is the portrayal of friendship in its various forms and transformations.

www.ingramcontent.com/pod-product-compliance
Lightning Source LLC
LaVergne TN
LVHW061604070526
838199LV00077B/7169